Top 13 Secrets To Success in Life & Business

Richard Branson

A Virgin Entrepreneur

EntrepreneurshipFacts.com

Warning-Disclaimer!

The purpose of this book is to educate and entertain. The author or publisher does not guarantee that anyone following the techniques, suggestions, tips, ideas, or strategies will become successful. The author and publisher shall have neither liability or responsibility to anyone with respect to any loss or damage caused or alleged to be caused, directly or indirectly by the information contained in this book.

All information contained within this book has been researched from reputable sources. If any information is found to be false, please contact the publisher, who will be happy to make corrections for future editions.

Follow EntrepreneurshipFacts on social media to stay updated with our free book promotions and increase your knowledge about business and successful people on a daily basis:

Instagram   Facebook   Twitter

Also check out our website for the latest facts and articles about business and entrepreneurship:

www.EntrepreneurshipFacts.com

Table of Contents

Introduction: 5

Short Biography 6

Quote # 1 – On Pitching Your Business 12

Quote # 2 – On Punctuality 19

Quote # 3 - On Failure 24

Quote # 4 - On Being Decisive 30

Quote # 5 - On Communication 36

Quote # 6 – On Fear 41

Quote # 7 – On Social Media 47

Quote # 8 – On Missed Opportunities 51

Quote # 9 – On Finding Opportunities 55

Quote # 10 – On Being Organized 59

Quote # 11 – On Taking Action 65

Quote #12 – On Treating Employees 71

Quote # 13 – On Taking Risks 80

Conclusion 86

Introduction:

Richard Charles Nicholas Branson was born on July 18, 1950 in Surrey, England. Toiled during his school years and dropped out at the young age of 16. This turn of events actually led to the origin of Virgin Records. Began in the industry of music, Branson's initiatives and enterprises spread into many different industries, leading to Branson's status as a billionaire. His original Virgin Group currently has over 200 different companies, including a space touring company, Virgin Galactic. Branson is well-known for his adventurous spirit, such as flying in a hot air balloon across the Atlantic Ocean.

Short Biography

When Richard Branson was born, his mother, Eve Branson, held a job as a flight attendant while his father, Edward James Branson, was an attorney. Richard's dyslexia made it difficult to learn and caused him problems in school. He attended Scaitcliffe School, an all-boys school, till the age of 13, and nearly failed out. After his struggles there, he switched to Stowe School, a boarding school in the town of Stowe, in Buckinghamshire, England.

The new school did not make Branson's struggle with schoolwork go away, so Branson dropped out of school at 16 and began a magazine named *Student*, engaging the youth subculture as a product designed for and also managed by young people. In 1966, the first issue of this magazine came out, supplying $8,000 dollars' worth of advertising. Since Branson was able to cover the costs by the advertising, he was able to distribute all 50,000 copies of this first run for free.

Three years later, in 1969, Branson found the drug and music industry all around where he lived in the London administrative district. To add to his magazine venture, Branson decided to add a new business to his repertoire. Calling his business "Virgin", he sold records by mail order. The business did fairly well, and made Branson enough money that he decided to start an actual record shop there in London on Oxford Street. The income from this shop allowed him to go on to found a recording studio by 1972 in the town of Oxfordshire.

With his own studio, he began to host recording artists. Mike Oldfield was the first to record for the Virgin Record's brand in 1973. Branson's group helped him record the "Tubular Bells" record. This record became popular immediately, and it remained on the UK's charts for 247 weeks. With this auspicious start, Branson's studio drew other groups, including the well-known Sex Pistols. When other groups such as the Rolling Stones, Genesis, and Culture Club also used his studios, his company became one of the top six record organizations in the world.

Branson's entrepreneur endeavors continued as he started Voyager Group, a tour organization in 1980 and Virgin Atlantic, an airline industry, four years later. Virgin Mega shops also gained popularity. However life was not all a bed of roses, and in 1992, Branson's Virgin business struggled financially, forcing Branson to sell the company for a billion dollars to Thorn EMI.

The loss devastated Branson, but he kept up his resolve to continue his presence in the music sector of business. Virgin Radio came into existence in 1993, and in '96, V2, another record company was formed. This company went on to include artists Tom Jones, Powder Finger, and others.

Now Virgin Group, owned by Branson, consists of over 200 businesses scattered throughout 30 nations including the United States, Canada, Australia, the United Kingdom, and countries in Europe, Asia and South Africa. His current holdings have expanded to include a mobile phone company, a luxury game preserve, a train company, and even Virgin Galactic, a space tourism company.

Branson's feats also include crossing the Atlantic and Pacific oceans by hot air balloon in 1987 and 1999, respectively, as well as breaking records on the Atlantic in 1986 in the Virgin Atlantic Challenger II. He received knighthood in 1999 for his entrepreneurial contributions.

In recent years, Branson has spent a lot of his energy focusing on space tourism. Joining with Scaled Composites, he began The Spaceship Company. In April of 2013, the company's goal of creating suborbital spacecraft made a huge stride forward as they test launched SpaceShipTwo. The test launch was a huge success, and Branson told NBC, "We're absolutely delighted that it broke the sound barrier on its very first flight, and that everything went so smoothly." As Branson made plans to do final testing that same year, he has sold over 500 tickets to travel on space voyages with Virgin Galactic.

Besides pursuing different business endeavors, Branson contributes to several charities, for example The Healthcare Foundation. Once Queen Elizabeth knighted him for being committed to the spirit of Britain and for his business competence, he was retitled Sir Richard Branson. As of 2016, Richard Branson net worth was $5.1 billion with the ranking number 286 on Forbes' list of billionaires, up from ranking number 330 in 2015.

This book will go on to examine some of Richard Branson's famous quotes and analyze the meaning and significance of each. Along with each quote is the real life story of how Richard Branson himself implements those same principles effectively in his life and business

Quote # 1 – On Pitching Your Business

"It is vitally important to present a clear, concise plan that investors can easily understand and repeat to their own people. In the first meeting, avoid overly complicated, numbers-laden presentations."

Quote context:

Interview with Carmine Gallo, a keynote speaker and communication coach as well as a contributor to Forbes in October of 2012.

Meaning of Quote:

Almost anywhere we turn, it seems that someone is trying to sell us something. Whether you're searching the internet or standing in line at the store, promotions and ads are all around you, vying for your attention. Some offers appeal to you, and cause you to contribute time, energy, or funds to the cause.

Think about it from the other side of the issue: when you want to advertise a product or idea that you are selling, do you know what you need to say to make others interested enough that they buy into your proposal? It is crucial to understand what steps you need to take to make others interested enough to consider your offer, as well as how to create a great pitch.

Lessons from Richard Branson

When Branson pitched his idea of starting Virgin Atlantic, his co-directors were not experts in the flight business, so Branson kept his terms simple, explaining in a concise and efficient way.

He encourages his fellow businessmen and leaders in the market:

> *"It is vitally important to present a clear, concise plan that investors can easily understand and repeat to their own people. In the first meeting avoid overly complicated, numbers-laden presentations."*

Branson shares some of his ideas regarding professional marketing and communicating in *Like a Virgin,* a book he authored. He states that in it, he discloses "secrets they won't teach you at business school" including how to communicate effectively and give demonstrations.

In the book, Branson goes on to explain that by keeping presentations outstanding and easy to understand, business owners can raise money even when financial circumstances make progress difficult. He recommends these five aspects to include in investment pitches:

- **What's in it for them?**

    "Occasionally, an entrepreneur hoping to launch their first business puts so much thought into the concept that he or she neglects the financial and legal plan—and unfortunately, this often becomes apparent early at a meeting, when an investor lack clarity on what exactly the proposed deal is going to look like."

    Branson realizes that investors want to know what benefit they will get out of the deal and when they might see income come in.

- **Be Definite**

"Winning the trust of an investor means demonstrating a thorough knowledge of your concept or industry and laying out a step-by-step plan for offering something that's new, innovative and will deliver healthy returns on their investment."

Branson discourages wishy-washy phrases like "It is hoped…" and "With some luck…" Rather, talk eye-to-eye, and confidently map out for them what results they can expect.

- **Be Unapologetically Disruptive**

   "Emphatically explain how your new company will give your customers a better deal than your competitors."

Don't be shy or timid. Be willing to disrupt the way things have always been done, just like Branson does. Use presentations, and clearly point out why your option is so much better than anything competitors can offer.

- **Demonstrate That Growth Is Maintainable.**

  "Nothing stays the same for long, so explain how you plan to tackle the inevitable technological changes and market shifts that are heading your way."

In order to sell your product, business leaders and investors want to see evidence so they can be sure that you understand the market. One way to help them feel confident and secure is to bring up the problem before they do, and explain how you've already thought through it and have answers. Make them see the problems they have with the old system as well, and then come in with the solution, rather than trying to sell them on the solution before they realize that they have a problem. Be specific in what goals your product will achieve, and how it will accomplish this for them. As Branson says, "Show prospective investors that you have found the right people to work at your new company."

Many times in pitches, the founders and CEO's want to look great and make others think that they can handle everything. In reality, sharing the stage and showing that you have a good work force proves to potential clients that you have bench strength.

Quote # 2 – On Punctuality

"Want to Be More Productive? Be More Punctual"

Quote context:

Written by Richard Branson and published on October 5, 2015

Meaning of Quote:

Punctuality not only shows our values and work ethic, it also can increase your productivity, personally or at a business level. The feeling of control that punctuality and following routine create in you can improve performance in general. The opposite is also true. When you run late, it is usually due to pressure which reduces your vitality and creative abilities, overall decreasing your efficiency.

Lessons from Richard Branson

While you may often hear that women and men who are prospering financially are also always on time, many may not see the connection between the two. To get a better grasp on it, think of the following examples. Have you ever accidentally arrived late to a meeting, and then felt embarrassed when your co-workers stare at you as you walk in after the meeting has already started? This messes up your good attitude, and everything is downhill from there. On the other hand, have you ever tried getting up 20 minutes earlier, and found that you seem to get done with everything quickly and feel very organized and on top of your day? When that happens, it seems like the rest of your day just falls into place without much effort.

Thus not only does punctuality allow us more time to do what we need to do, it can also affect the overall way we see ourselves and feel about the day.

Richard Branson states, "If you want to be more productive, then start at the start: get there on time. Whether it is a meeting, a flight, an appointment or a date, ensure you are there when you say you will be there."

Being punctual and choosing to arrive when you promised to, in essence, is being respectful of other people's time. Next time you have a meeting or an appointment, try showing up 10 minutes early, and see how you feel.

Branson commented, "Being on time is respectful to your hosts and also means you can effectively manage your day. Once you get behind, it is hard to catch back up again. Being punctual doesn't mean rushing around the whole time. It simply means organizing your time effectively."

Branson admitted that if he is running late, sometimes he will begin to run in order to try to make it in time for a consultation or conference with the media.

"Of course, everything doesn't always go to plan. It isn't always possible to be on time, but it is always possible to try. When I find myself running late, I will often quite literally resort to running. I was in New York a few years ago and our Virgin Unite events took a little longer than expected. The Manhattan traffic was typically hectic, and I found myself trapped on the other side of town, needing to get to Fox News in time for a live interview. As I peered out of the car window into the immobile queues, I jumped out of the front seat and sprinted down Sixth Avenue. I spotted the Fox sign, hopped across the lobby and began banging on the window. I made it with a minute to spare"

He added:

"Being on time doesn't mean working to a strict, rigid schedule. It means being an effective delegator, organizer and communicator. If it isn't going to be possible for me to make an appointment, make that clear and apologize. If possible, find one of the team who will find it useful to attend on your behalf, and then ask them to feed back to you. If it really isn't possible to be on time, call ahead."

Quote # 3 - On Failure

"Failure and rejection are an inevitable part of business, and how you deal with them will ultimately affect your success. The ability to cope with and learn from failure and rejection can be practiced and honed along the way. Some people are better at it than others."

Meaning of Quote:

While failure is painful, it is also crucially important to many aspects of life. It makes a great teacher, as it chips away overloading circumstances, humbles us, and allows us to learn sacred truths.

Without failure, we would not be able to empathize as well with others, make as good decisions, or accomplish as many things. Failure helps us overcome, and make aspirations of reaching the stars and moon.

Only through failure do we learn life's most valuable and important lessons.

Lessons from Richard Branson

It would not be exaggerated to say that entrepreneurs experience failure on a daily basis. Under these circumstances, genuine businessmen accept it and go on to regroup, taking into account what happened, and beginning over again. How do you make the call whether or not your business is not going to work out or there is too much opposition, and decide to move on?

Branson's brand name has brought numerous businesses into being in sectors including music, travel, telecoms, medical, monetary services, and fitness. With so many businesses, it is not surprising that he has also encountered a few failures.

> *"We've never been 100% sure that any of the businesses we've started at Virgin were going to be successful,"* Branson replied. *"But over 45 years, we've always stood by our motto: 'Screw it, let's do it'. While this attitude has helped us build hundreds of companies, it hasn't always resulted in success."*

He describes one of the company's greatest blunders, attempting to invade the soft drink sector with Virgin Cola.

> *"We felt confident that we could beat the competition, but it turned out that we hadn't thought things through. We weren't prepared for the size or ferocity of Coca-Cola response, which included a steep increase in their marketing budget and pressure on distributors not to work with us."*

Although they had fierce competition, Branson still feels that the reason the business failed was due to their own failure to keep the rules they had established. He explains it this way:

> *"Virgin only enters an industry when we think we can offer consumers something strikingly different that will disrupt the market, but there wasn't really an opportunity to do that in the soft drinks market. People were already getting a product that they liked, at a price they were happy to pay. Virgin Cola just wasn't different enough."*

He says:

> *"Failure and rejection are an inevitable part of business, and how you deal with them will ultimately affect your success. The ability to cope with and learn from failure and rejection can be practiced and honed along the way. Some people are better at it than others."*

> *"We have had many great successes at Virgin, but we've also experienced a number of failures. Every time something hasn't worked out as we hoped it would, we have picked ourselves up, looked at what went wrong, and learned from our mistakes."*

Another of the failures that helped to shape Branson happened early on in his life, when he was not able to persuade an important publication house that they should purchase *Student Magazine*. Instead of presenting his business as something to meet their desires, concentrating on specific aspects of distribution techniques, Branson explained to them his entire dream for making Student into an array of businesses, including magazines, tour organizations and financial institutions. The company was overwhelmed, and chose not to purchase the business. However this failure led to future successes as Branson determined to set out and do everything he dreamed, founding companies that lived up to his beliefs.

Looking at what has happened several decades later, Virgin has expanded to include more companies and sectors that Branson ever dreamed of as a young man.

While Branson's thoughts on failure are very practical, they might be hard for some to swallow, since many have grown up thinking that failure is taboo and should be shunned at all costs.

Quote # 4 - On Being Decisive

"As an entrepreneur, you'll often be faced with tough calls, but you have to think about what's best for your business and what's best for your staff."

Meaning of Quote:

Whiles owning a business can be satisfying to the owner, it also presents the great challenge of making difficult decisions on a daily basis. Furthermore, not only that you have to make decisions, you are also responsible to the consequences of those decisions you made. Others may be willing to give you advice, but in the end, you are liable.

Others may think your decision looks ridiculous or even unfair to your staff, customers, business partners, contacts or associates. However, if you think the decision is what best for your business then you will have to grit your teeth and go through with the decision you have made, hoping for the best.

Lessons from Richard Branson

The larger a startup grows, the bigger and weightier results any potential decisions will have become. There is more and more at stake that could be lost if a decision is unwise.

The challenge of balancing attachment to the business you've started from scratch to the need to make somewhat risky decisions for the good or your business is a very real one, especially if the choice seems to go against the grain of the business.

Richard Branson talks about one the most difficult decisions he has made, the choice to sell Virgin Records.

"It was our baby, we'd built it up from the ground to the position of the world's most successful independent label,"

he then says.

"As an entrepreneur, you'll often be faced with tough calls, but you have to think about what's best for your business and what's best for your staff. At the time of the Virgin Records sale our first airline, Virgin Atlantic, was under intense pressure from British Airways and their dirty tricks campaign. We needed funds to protect ourselves and hire a legal team to bring an end to their underhand behavior. While we would have loved to continue running both companies, it seemed more likely that they would both continue to prosper if we sold Records."

Sometimes, a business' will fall or remain intact based on a very courageous choice the owner will make, as in Branson's case.

While sentimentally, it is very difficult to sell a business, especially thinking about how the move could affect staff, allowing yourself to make decisions based on your sentimental feelings could be the downfall of your business.

Entrepreneurs have to learn to cope with the unknowns and the possibility of making a wrong decision. It is at these moments that their true colors and strength shines through.

Branson explains:

> *"While fear can act as an energy and, to a certain extent, exert a positive influence over your entrepreneurial spirit, regrets rarely help you. Entrepreneurs should view failure in a more positive light, it happens to everyone and there's no shame in trying something that doesn't come off."*

> *"Failure is all part of the learning process, we don't spend time dwelling over the demise of Virgin Cola, for example, we use it to inform our future decisions and make the brand stronger."*

One of the hardest parts of establishing a business from the ground up is when you have to lay off quality workers in order to enhance the overall company, letting these reliable workers know that there is no longer a job for them in your organization.

Once you have decided that such a step is necessary, however, it is important to act quickly, because putting it off will not be helpful. Maintaining authority and clear communication with staff and managers, especially in these times, and keeping these people in mind as you make difficult decisions regarding job termination can help to make a difficult process a little smoother.

Quote # 5 - On Communication

"Communication Is the Most Important Skill Any Leader Can Possess"

Quote context

A Blog Post : http://www.virgin.com/richard-branson/my-top-10-quotes-on-communication

Meaning of Quote:

This quote is straight forward. Whether you're speaking national politics, business, the military or sports activities, high quality communicators pull ahead as the best and most competent leaders. They have clear and stable principles, and back up those principles by what they say. Their teammates follow their lead and admire them. In a similar way, clear communication is vital for your business to reach higher levels of accomplishment.

Communication happens when information is transmitted from one person to another. This can take place by vocal speech, written words (including books, websites, e-mails magazines, etc.), through visual information (such as charts, maps, or graphs), and nonverbally (through body language and tone of voice).

While communication is only one aspect of being a good leader, it, along with knowing how to organize, lead, plan, control, and find the right staff are crucial aspects of running a business.

Besides this, the business owner must focus on the basics of business, perfecting their abilities to discipline, position the company strategically, control their principles, act responsibly, and empower their employees.

Lessons from Richard Branson

Richard Branson stated that communication is "an art" in one of his blog posts. This assessment hits the nail on the head. Scientific reasoning can explain why certain strategies are more successful and others less so, but communication is different, more of an art. Like with any type of art, practice is crucial to sharpen your skills and master the ability.

Branson quotes Brian Tracy, a business writer, stating:

> *"Communication is a skill that you can learn. It's like riding a bicycle or typing. If you're willing to work at it, you can rapidly improve the quality of every part of your life."*

Branson believes that, "Communication makes the world go round. It facilitates human connections, and allows us to learn, grow and progress. It's not just about speaking or reading, but understanding what is being said – and in some cases what is not being said. Communication is the most important skill any leader can possess. We have certainly relied on it to drive the success of the Virgin story. In appreciation of the art of communication."

Richard Branson lists the following as his top 10 quotes on the topic of communication:

10. "Write to be understood, speak to be heard, read to grow." – Lawrence Clark Powell

9. "I remind myself every morning: Nothing I say this day will teach me anything. So if I'm going to learn, I must do it by listening." – Larry King

8. "Kind words can be short and easy to speak, but their echoes are truly endless." – Mother Theresa

7. "Storytellers, by the very act of telling, communicate a radical learning that changes lives and the world: telling stories is a universally accessible means through which people make meaning." – Chris Cavanaugh

6. "Communication is a skill that you can learn. It's like riding a bicycle or typing. If you're willing to work at it, you can rapidly improve the quality of every part of your life." – Brian Tracy

5. "I speak to everyone in the same way, whether he is the garbage man or the president of the university." – Albert Einstein

4. "Good communication is as stimulating as black coffee, and just as hard to sleep after." – Anne Morrow Lindbergh

3. "The art of communication is the language of leadership." – James Humes

2. "Most of the successful people I've known are the ones who do more listening than talking." – Bernard Baruch

1. "Two monologues do not make a dialogue." – Jeff Daly

Quote # 6 – On Fear

"Don't Be Afraid Of Fear"

Meaning of Quote:

Many people seek to avoid risk for fear of losing money or becoming poor. Decisions based on fear are not the best type of decisions, and should not be the final determining factor in the decisions we make. Top on the list of what people fear are the following:

- Fear of failure.
- Fear that they will not succeed if they try something new.
- Fear that if they undertake something they feel passionate about, they will not be able to "make it".
- Fear often prevents people from pursuing their dreams

Fearing failure is not an easy fear to overcome, but when you have enough courage to try even knowing you could fail, you have the potential to achieve greater things than you could otherwise.

This prevalent fear of failure also causes people to turn down great opportunities, fearing that they will not be able to succeed. This fear paralyzes and those in its grip often fear taking any type of risks.

While fear of failure is one of the most common fears people face, many also fear losing love, or losing financial stability or their job. The thought of shame and ridicule stirs up fear in the hearts of many, as does the thought of rejection or any type of negative feedback. Many fear losing respect from others. All these fears hold people back and keep them from taking the risks that could help them succeed.

Lessons from Richard Branson

Richard Branson had to overcome his fear of failure to make the decisions necessary to succeed. At age 16, he dared to start his first business. Choice after choice, he showed bravery to be able to set himself apart as a famous adventurer, entrepreneur and philosopher. As Virgin Group's founder, he also ranks among the wealthiest in the world. While his fame and riches are impressive, they are not what have set him apart as phenomenal, but rather his drive to influence the world in a positive way.

His willingness to take risks and live his life to its maximum potential has inspired millions of individuals around the world. Since childhood he has dreamed big and made impressive innovations, but there have also been times when he has struggled and faced failed attempts. Even so, many of his failures have given rise to great achievements.

Failure is a necessary part of being an entrepreneur, and Branson shows through his life that risk-taking is a necessary part of accomplishing your dreams. The following quotes point out Branson's positive outlook that has allowed him to reach the success he is enjoying today:

> *"The brave may not live forever – but the cautious do not live at all."*

Abraham Lincoln, president of the United States, once stated, "In the end, it's not the years in your life that count. It's the life in your years." In other words, enjoy every minute of your life and live it to the fullest. Don't be so scared you avoid taking risks and trying new things.

In fact, if you find that you fear doing something, all the more reason to try it. Doing breathtaking things is one of the things that make life worth living. If you want to rise to the top, you cannot be very careful and shy. Keep pushing yourself to your full potential and don't trap yourself by fear.

"Screw it; let's just do it."

This quote can be helpful to repeat to yourself, reminding yourself to run for the things you are hesitant to do. Then you will not regret chances you had that you failed to take.

The wise and successful individuals have gained their knowledge and experience through making mistake after mistake. Take what life gives you and run with it. Our world is exhilarating, with hit and miss opportunities all the time. Don't allow yourself or others to deprive you of these chances.

"You don't learn to walk by following rules. You learn by doing, and by falling over."

Like a child learns to walk through repeatedly trying and falling down, we too need to take chances and be daring. Many times, venturing off the beaten trail can lead to discovering new opportunities we would never have seen otherwise. Some things that once were just crazy dreams have now become reality, like the airplane. Many of the most amazing human achievements have been the result of pursuing insane dreams.

Failure is part of the process of maturing for humans. In order to rise, you must fall first. Don't be deceived into thinking that failure is final. Keep fighting, working, and don't throw in the towel. A strong mind requires holding onto a positive outlook even when others try to fill your mind with pessimistic thoughts.

Quote # 7 – On Social Media

"In the past few years, social media has revolutionized the way businesses interact with customers, making it easier to market new products and maintain a brand's image. By now it's clear that platforms like Facebook, Twitter and Google+ should be an essential part of customer service."

Quote context

Sir Richard Branson addresses the media during a rebranding launch, which saw Virgin Australia replace Virgin Blue and V Australia, at Sydney Airport on May 4, 2011 in Sydney, Australia.

Meaning of Quote:

While in the past, a company could get by without a website, now developing a website for the business and promoting it is crucial. Social media websites are also important to having a successful business and brand name, and Facebook and Twitter can be necessary to maintain your company's edge on the market. Without dynamic social media, a company risks losing opportunities for marketing and advertising.

Using social media makes giving and receiving feedback much easier. Customers can easily inform you of issues they have, or express their opinions and give feedback regarding products and services the company offers. These platforms allow companies to know what complaints clients have, and address them in a timely way, reassuring customers that any problems will be resolved.

Lessons from Richard Branson

When it comes to using social media, Richard Branson has six tips. He shares how his company Virgin Unite is making the best of the social media era to spread their message. While these tips are especially geared to non-profits, they are applicable to other businesses as well, and good to keep in mind when attempting to market using social media.

1. Share stories. "People respond to stories, not data."
2. Innovate. "Experiment with new ways of telling stories and make the most of all the new tools out there like Tumblr and Storify."
3. Use the right medium. "Match your content to different platforms and audiences."
4. Tell the truth. "Don't pretend you're something you're not."
5. Work as a team. "Collaborate with people and organizations who are fighting for the same cause."
6. Enjoy yourself. "Work should be fun and making work fun brings success."

Put these principles into effect in your own life and business. Successful executives are willing to engage with others over social media themselves, rather than just delegating the task to others. Once when a Forbes contributor, Carmine Gallo, who was spending a day with Richard Branson, was impressed to notice that Branson carried a smartphone and sent out tweets from time to time. One example of this was when a marketing manager showed Branson a photo of one of Virgin's employees. Branson quickly responded, "Send me the photo. I'll think of a funny caption and I'll post it." As a famous CEO, Richard Branson has over 3.5 million who follow him; remarkably, the majority of the tweets he posts himself. Branson also writes his own blog posts.

Quote # 8 – On Missed Opportunities

"Business opportunities are like buses, there's always another one coming."

Quote context

As a reply to a question on his 'Challenge Richard Quest.

Meaning of Quote:

Richard Branson, the business expert, has certainly had his share of opportunities. When it comes to opportunities, it's important to remember that if one opportunity falls through, another one will likely come along if we keep hoping and keep our eyes open. If one pursuit is not working out, it is important to know when to let it go and start on the next one.

Lessons from Richard Branson

When Branson was questioned in a 'Challenge Richard Quest', he identified certain concepts he let go of because he didn't find them to be ideal. He explains:

> *"I'm fortunate to have had thousands of business ideas come across my lap. And as someone that loves to say yes, yes, yes, you can imagine just how hard it is for me to turn down anything that shows promise. But business is a game of opportunity and sometimes opportunity simply strikes at the wrong time."*

> *"Trivial Pursuit is perhaps the biggest business idea that got away from me. I got a call one day in the early 80s from a friend in Canada, who had become obsessed by the new board game and told me it was going to be the next big thing. The developers invited us to travel to Quebec and seal a deal to distribute the game globally. However, we were incredibly busy with Virgin Records at the time, and due to work commitments I ended up having to postpone the trip. By the time I was ready, they had sold the game to another company, who went on to sell hundreds of millions of copies."*

Going on further, he pointed out,

> *"Similarly, we also had the opportunity to bring the businesses now known as JetBlue and Ryanair under the Virgin brand. But at the respective times, the deals just weren't right. Business is funny like*

that – sometimes you're in the right place at the right time; other days you're feeling brave and more willing to seize the day; then there are times when you've got to protect your existing business interests."

In conclusion, he said,

"But you can't be greedy, and I have absolutely no regrets about any of these missed opportunities. After all, opportunities are like buses – there's always another one coming!"

Quote # 9 – On Finding Opportunities

"The best businesses come from people's bad personal experiences. If you just keep your eyes open, you're going to find something that frustrates you, and then you think, well I could maybe do it better than it's being done,' and there you have a business."

Quote Context

During an hour long Interview hosted by *CreativeLive* in a daily interview series *30 Days of Genius*.

Meaning of Quote:

Talk to any successful entrepreneur, or any professional with a positive attitude, and you'll find one key trait in common: all of them have a unique mentality that allows them to handle challenges differently. Rather than seeing problems as burdensome dilemmas, they see problems as opportunities--opportunities to learn, grow, improve, or adjust in a way that leaves them better off than before the problem existed.

There's an old saying "There are no problems – only opportunities." Too often we focus on the problems and fail to realize the opportunities right in front of us. To turn things around, start by focusing on finding a solution. When you think of problems you will only attract more problems. When you think of solutions, you'll attract solutions and opportunities.

Lessons from Richard Branson

While bad experiences are often something we avoid, Richard Branson has built his whole business by allowing his frustrations to motivate him to push to find solutions.

Ever since his first business endeavor, Student Magazine, he has utilized the principle. His magazine took into consideration the fact that a lot of journals and school magazines were boring, and tried to offer a solution—an interesting magazine designed for young people.

Applying that same principle, Branson has come to head 400 companies, anywhere from banking institutions to airlines, to record stores, to space travel, to fitness clubs, and much more. Branson claims that each of these originally resulted from some area of frustration.

Branson encourages business owners to go beyond simply being able to identify negative experiences to channel that frustration to develop a plan to help change the market. He states, "If you can improve people's lives, you have a business."

Sometimes your business concept might be taken already or some other company might be promoting a similar service or product. How do you know whether or not you still have margin to succeed or if there are too many competitors? Branson shares his insight:

> *"People think, 'Well, everything's been thought of,' but actually, all of the time, there are gaps in the market here and gaps in the market there."*

Branson has discovered that many times it's just doing things a little different and a little better than can be the beginning of a successful business.

Quote # 10 – On Being Organized

"I have always lived my life by making lists. These vary from lists of people to call, lists of ideas, lists of companies to set up, lists of people who can make things happen. I also have lists of topics to blog about, lists of tweets to send, and lists of upcoming plans"

Quote Context

In his book "The Virgin Way: Everything I Know About Leadership

Meaning of Quote:

Lists help us stay organized. If you're seeking to achieve, writing items down can be a big help because it forces you to analyze all that you hope to get done and decide how you are going to accomplish it. Also the feeling of crossing items off your list can help you feel accomplished and allow you to enjoy your successes more than when you merely race from one achievement to the next without taking time to think. This feeling allows you to gain courage to go forward rather than feeling that all your to-do items are weighing hopelessly on you.

Lessons from Richard Branson

What would happen to Richard Branson if he tried to function without lists? He himself claims that lists greatly help him in life, as he writes down tasks he needs to do, checks his list often, and marks off the tasks he completes.

Branson claims this strategy, which doesn't even require advanced technology but rather simple notebooks that anyone can buy at the store, has contributed to his success. Not only does this method not involve advanced technology, but it doesn't require a highly intelligent technique. The only major skill that it involves is being able to decipher your own personal handwriting!

What does Branson put onto his lists? And what can we learn by observing this discipline in his life? Branson describes the four lists he keeps in *Losing My Virginity*, his autobiography:

List of people to call: One of Branson's strengths is to be able to win people to his cause and motivate them to move the same direction he is going. Sometimes, it's Branson who changes his direction so he lines up with them. Whichever way it goes, Branson feels that listing out the people he wants to call is an important element of keeping everyone on the same team. He points out, "Each day I work through those lists and that sequence of calls propels me forward."

Lists of ideas: Irregardless of whether an idea comes out of Richard Branson's imagination or from someone he meets, he writes it down quickly. That way he can revisit the lists to make sure he hasn't neglected anything or forgotten any great idea. Of course, many times an idea doesn't seem quite so brilliant when you look back on it later, but there are good ideas often enough that it is worth it to write them down.

Lists of things people say: Branson doesn't just write down remarks CEOs make, but the significant comments from all those he comes into contact with. Since he takes notes on most phone calls and each meeting he attends, he is able to keep track of different people's points of view. He has found that a nice side note of recording what people say is that it forces him to give close attention to others' thoughts and ideas.

Lists of people who can make things happen: Branson also keeps a list of influential individuals that it pays to keep in touch with. That way he can ensure that these people are kept up to speed on what is going on, and he can keep tabs on what ideas they are developing. Maintaining good relationships with such movers and shakers is one of the best ways he spends his time.

While keeping lists like Branson does may not make you a billionaire, it can help you keep your life focused around the most important things. If you begin to make lists in the above four categories, you can improve your track record of staying focused on what you are doing.

Another aspect of Branson's list-making is that he keeps all his old lists. When one notebook is full, he keeps it, from time to time consulting an old notebook and finding an idea that merits being passed over again. Although he has years' worth of bookcases of notebooks, he finds it helpful to look over them to glean insights.

As you follow Branson's pattern of making lists, you can keep better track of your time so you will have more time to invest in deciding what is actually important. With this added bit of self-discipline, you can keep from forgetting those things you hope to accomplish from day to day.

Quote # 11 – On Taking Action

" If somebody offers you an amazing opportunity but you are not sure you can do it, say yes – then learn how to do it later"

Meaning of Quote:

If you like an idea, go for it, and figure out how to make it work as you go. Don't be afraid of what could happen.

Lessons from Richard Branson

Because of Richard Branson's opportunistic approach to life and his drive and passion, he has amassed wealth. Branson's vocabulary doesn't include the word "can't", leading to the nickname of "Dr. Yes"; this attitude allows him to experiment with novel ideas and to try new things. As he takes on these challenges in this bold and daring way, he has attained success more than he could have imagined.

Rules have never stopped Richard—his determination overrides rules and public opinion. When he faces obstacles, he overcomes them in order to continue pursuing the adventure he has begun. He showed his persistence and determination when he first tried to start a business and people were critical of his attempts to start up the Student magazine. They argued that at such a young age and with no experience, he couldn't help but fail. He didn't let their opinions get him down, and went on boldly interviewing famous people that more established magazines sought for their publications. As he fought the odds, he kept on without giving up, and eventually succeeded and worked his way up in life. That same zeal and passion have led to worldwide publicity for his Virgin Airlines Company.

One characteristic of Richard Branson that gives him resilience is that he does not fear rejection, either personally, or when it comes to his business. In Screw It, Let's Do It, his well-known book, Branson describes how he didn't give up on purchasing Necker Island even when his first offer was denied. Although the island had been put up for sale at £3 million, he made an offer of £150,000. The end deal was £180,000, and while Branson didn't have cash on hand, he borrowed from his family and raised the needed money.

Another daring thing that Branson did was to buy back all of Virgin's shares when the Virgin Group shares were rapidly falling. Although by doing this, he took all the risk onto himself, this also allowed the company to return to being a private company once more.

Branson holds that a person should do what is necessary to succeed in life, and to act on the brilliant ideas that they come up with. Many in the past have chosen to act on great ideas, and even though they lacked resources, were able to start companies of their own. When an individual has the "do it" attitude, they don't give up when faced with hard circumstances, and they don't give in to discouragement as they follow their dreams. Now, the internet provides those with low or nonexistent resources more opportunities to try and succeed. If you are determined, don't say "can't" or give in to fear, the biggest enemy of those trying for success.

Having fun on the job is another factor that Richard Branson values. When you dislike your job, you feel miserable, and your performance drops as well. When possible, pursue your dreams and aspirations instead of merely taking any job you can find that does not give satisfaction or fulfillment. When you have to work at a job you dislike or can't put your heart into, try to separate work and the rest of your life as much as possible so that your feelings about work don't carry over into the rest of your life as well. Look on the bright side of things, and make the best of your circumstances instead of complaining and bemoaning the things you can't change. Whether you enjoy your job or not, seek to have fun while you work.

While being a billionaire greatly increases Richard Branson's popularity, keep in mind that he didn't turn into a billionaire by accident. Rather, by zealous and passionate work, he has attained what he is today. While even Branson will confess that many of his life circumstances have been lucky, his tenacity and hard work have led to success.

Richard Branson's life shows us that in order to attain success in business and life, a person not only needs to have big dreams, but to be able to follow his dreams with bravery and passion. Instead of giving in to fear, individuals must face their fears head-on, boldly doing what it takes as they seek to follow their dreams.

Quote #12 – On Treating Employees

"The companies that look after their people are the companies that do really well. I'm sure we'd like a few other attributes, but that would be the most important one."

Quote Context

From a 2005 American Express event, via Business Pundit

Meaning of Quote:

Happiness fosters being successful in business. This point has been verified by a study which showed that happiness causes people to work more effectively. The University of Warwick carried out research that revealed staff members were more effective when they felt happy at their workplace.

Since Richard Branson sees that having staff members who are happy is crucial. He runs his business by the principle of putting staff first, clients second and your investors third. Customer service is not all that matters when it comes to making clients happy, but the staff as well. Richard Branson explains, "If you look after your staff, they'll look after your customers. It's that simple." Happy workers are more motivated to use their time to successfully work with others and develop strategies that will be good for the business. As a result, when your staff are happy, they will make your clients happy, and in turn your clients will be happy to pay for your service, which ultimately makes your investors happy.

Lessons from Richard Branson

Customer service was the key to Branson's ability to make Virgin into such a huge multinational corporation. From Virgin Mobile to Virgin Atlantic and everything in between, Branson shares that each branch of the corporation displays strong devotion to their customers. When Branson buys a new business, he will not allow it to be called by the Virgin name till it conforms to the high quality level of customer service that he expects from his employees.

However even with his devotion to excellent customer service, the customer is not the most important; rather Virgin's employees are the top priority for the company. While longstanding business wisdom seems to say otherwise, Branson has had such success with this model that he wonders why more companies haven't adopted this employee-centric approach to management.

During an interview, Branson told Eric Schurenberg, Inc.'s editor-in-chief and president, "It should go without saying, if the person who works at your company is 100 percent proud of the brand and you give them the tools to do a good job and they are treated well, they're going to be happy."

Branson takes this seriously, even visiting different departments in different areas, and talking personally with the staff. Branson believes that there is a direct cause/effect relationship, and that having happy staff members translates directly into happy customers. On the other side of the equation, an unhappy staff member can damage the company's reputation not just for one customer, but potentially for many.

"If the person who works at your company is not appreciated, they are not going to do things with a smile," Branson reminds us. When a company fails to treat employees in a caring way, they risk losing customers because of delivering low-quality service. In order to avoid this, Branson has made a point to make sure that Virgin puts the workforce first, followed by the customers, and finally the investors.

Richard Branson sums it up this way: "Effectively, in the end, shareholders do well, the customers do better, and your staff remains happy."

What steps does Richard Branson take to make his employees happy? He suggests that well-designed office spaces that allow for natural light is a first step. Branson encourages building inspirational jobs, a good strategy for rewarding good work, and emphasizing maintaining employee health. To this end, Virgin offers a special healthcare deal, Virgin Pulse, "a business that is focused on helping companies to encourage their employees to be more active through a reward program."

He believes that you should "Train people well enough so they can leave, treat them well enough so they don't want to." A company's staff members are a vital resource to the organization, and therefore it is important to acknowledge the work and effort they invest in the company. Be sure to have fun while celebrating their successes. This spurs them on to work harder and do their jobs to the best of their ability.

Additionally, Virgin has developed an adjustable working policy that allows employees to work at whatever location they choose, and at their own hours.

> *"It wasn't easy to put this system in place: Our team invested in research beforehand to make sure it was workable, and once we all agreed, we had to encourage a change of culture across our offices. Yet that was a small price to pay, because it's what our employees wanted, and we knew that*

demonstrating respect and trust in our employees would boost their happiness levels, and in turn, their productivity and creativity."

But Branson knows that happy and healthy employees can't be done merely through developing policies. In order to truly succeed at this goal, members of the staff must feel they have an investment in the company. One way to do this is for employees to own stock in the company where they work. Other companies help their staff to invest psychologically in the business.

One way to help staff members feel invested is to encourage them to recognize and celebrate the ways your company is unique and extraordinary. Another important consideration is to help them track with your company's purpose, and to provide them links or means of following how the company is doing with meeting its goals. Some companies focus on engaging with clients in order to help their employees feel invested. When this is the case, allow staff to take leadership roles and interact with clients in this way. If you don't know where to start, think through the different departments of your company, and note which one has the happiest employees. Then think about what is going well there and what factors are contributing to their happiness. Once you identify these factors, you can seek to implement them in other departments.

Be sure to celebrate the successes that the company and individual employees make in fun and exciting ways, even if this means (as was the case once with Branson's company) that the police officers have to shut down a pirate-themed party because of complaints about the noise level.

Branson explains:

> "We had a great time! But the next day we found ourselves on the front page of the local papers,

because the neighbors had called the authorities to complain about the sound of our steel drums on the roof terrace, which perhaps played a little later into the evening than they should have. While we did apologize for the inconvenience, that was a night nobody in the office will forget, and it did wonders for reviving our team spirit."

Quote # 13 – On Taking Risks

"You've got to take risks if you're going to succeed. I would much rather ask forgiveness than permission."

Meaning of Quote:

Taking risks is scary, whether you're going all-in during a friendly game of poker or quitting your long-time career to pursue one of your promising business ideas. Most people tend to avoid risks when possible, because inaction is often safer than action, but most successful people will tell you they got to where they are because they were willing to take risks no one else was -- whether that meant developing a product nobody else thought would work or investing a sum of money when everyone else thought that was crazy.

Lessons from Richard Branson

Many people think of Richard Branson as a brave and daring entrepreneur, a daredevil who has taken and absorbed risk in business just as he has in his exciting adventures of kite surfing in the English Channel or flying over the ocean in a hot air balloon.

While this impression has a degree of truth to it, it's easy to overlook the fact that the same risks could easily have resulted in catastrophe, and nearly did so several times.

While Virgin Records holds a place in enterprising lore, what about Virgin Brides? Does anyone even know or hear about the bridal shop chain (that has since been abandoned) that Richard Branson once established? Then there was Virgin Cola, and Branson's attempt to overthrow Coca-Cola's industry, even driving a tank into Times Square to announce his intent (which over time Branson has come to consider one of his worst business mistakes).

While Branson and his companies have made some mistakes and experienced some failures, Branson doesn't concentrate on these things. He remembers how, after dropping out of high school, his headmaster wrote him and said, "Congratulations, Branson. I predict that you will either go to prison or become a millionaire." While that prediction was lacking several zeros, it serves as a reminder that failure is not final. In 1992, Branson sold his record label for a billion dollars, and used the money to protect his airline company, Virgin Atlantic, against a financial threat, and to bring his Virgin empire to include 400 businesses.

Entrepreneur Magazine interviewed Richard Branson, and some excerpts from this interview point out Branson's approach on taking risks:

Entrepreneur: "How did those early stumbles shape Virgin as a company?"

Branson:

"In Britain, people who try things and then fail are actually well-respected. People like the underdog. If you go back to my adventure times, generally speaking, we failed on most of my adventures the first time. In attempting to bring back the Blue Riband [an award given to a ship for crossing the Atlantic Ocean in record time] in Great Britain, we created the boat the Atlantic Challenger in 1985. All was going very well until we sank 300 miles from the U.K., and were rescued by a banana boat.

"And the next year, we picked ourselves up and tried again and succeeded. Interestingly, if we had succeeded the first time, I think it would've been a big story, but not the massive story it turned into. At the time, we had just launched Virgin Atlantic; we were trying to put it on the map, and we *jokingly took a full-page advert with a picture of the hull sticking out of the water saying, 'Next time, Richard, take the plane.' But it was things like that, where we tried and failed, that put Virgin on the map, gave it a sexier image than our bigger rivals, and turned us into an adventurous company and brand."*

While billionaires don't necessarily take more risks than others do, they have a tendency, when taking risks, to analyze beforehand whether they can live with the end results of whatever happens, whether they are negative or positive. Branson was one such person. He took multiple risks throughout his life, leading to his present success. Crossing the ocean in a hot air balloon, as he did in 1987 and 1991, could have had disastrous results. While many would avoid the risk all together, Branson dared to do it. Likewise he founded a Spaceship Company, working his way into the space tourism business. People flocked to the idea, with over 800 purchasing tickets. While a few of these 800 demanded that their tickets be refunded later after SpaceShipTwo crashed in the Mojave Desert in California, this didn't deter Branson. Stellar leaders realize that some of their attempts will be great successes, while others may result in loss. However they move forward and don't let fear keep them from trying.

Conclusion

Richard Branson is different than many billionaires. He is famous around the globe, enthusiastically supporting humanitarian causes, and has a daring spirit that leads to such exciting ventures as crossing the ocean in a hot air balloon. Branson's business understanding is shown by his net worth of $5.1 billion, but that doesn't stop him from enjoying life to the full, and even going on an escapade every now and then.

As can be seen, Branson's life is very informative, and sometimes amusing. Therefore, do not wait till you are successful to enjoy life. Start now, and see where life takes you!

Finally, if you enjoyed this book, then I'd like to ask you for a favor, would you be kind enough to leave a review for this book on Amazon? Tell us what you like or dislike and what we can improve. Your feedbacks will be greatly appreciated!

https://www.amazon.com/dp/B01LY4YHB7

Also follow EntrepreneurshipFacts on social media to stay updated with our new books and increase your knowledge about business and successful people on a daily basis:

Instagram   Facebook   Twitter

Check out our website for the latest facts and articles about business and entrepreneurship:

www.EntrepreneurshipFacts.com

More books by Entrepreneurship Facts

101 Entrepreneurial Facts About 10 of The Most Successful BILLIONAIRES That Can Inspire You: What you can learn from their successes

The Real Life RICH DAD & The Lessons He Taught

ROBERT KIYOSAKI about Money

Warren Buffett - 41 Fascinating Facts about Life & Investing Philosophy: The Lessons From A Legendary Investor

Elon Musk - Top 10 Business Lessons Through An Inspiring Life Of A Visionary Entrepreneur:

www.ingramcontent.com/pod-product-compliance
Lightning Source LLC
Chambersburg PA
CBHW060406190526
45169CB00002B/783